All Rise: Church Staff

Building an Effective Ministry Staff

1

All Rise: Church Staffing

Building an Effective Ministry Staff

© 2013 by Dr. William E. Flippin Sr, & James McWhorter

All rights reserved. No part of this book may be reproduced or transmitted in any form or my any means, electronic of mechanical, including photocopying, recording, or by any information storage or retrieval system, without written permission from authors, except for the inclusion of quotations in a review.

Cover design by W. T. Dandridge, LEDNEW Marketing & Promotions Inc.

(Original work published 2012)

Building an Effective Ministry Staff

Dedications...

From: Dr. William E. Flippin, Sr.

To: My wife of almost 40 years, Mrs. Sylvia Taylor Flippin, who while I was administering and managing the church, she was holding it together at home.

From: Dr. James McWhorter

To: My wife Margaret of 41 years, for your unwavering love and devotion, and to my children, James III, Eric and Camille.

Building an Effective Ministry Staff

Building an Effective Ministry Staff

Table of Contents

All Rise: Church Staffing

Building an Effective Ministry Staff

Building an Effective Ministry Staff

Building an Effective Ministry Staff

Building an Effective Ministry Staff

Introduction

Let me start off by being absolutely honest. When I accepted this call from God and prayed to one day pastor a striving and growing church, I never imagined that I would have to master Human Resources. In my past church membership (before becoming a pastor), I always knew the church had a secretary who would prepare bulletins, answer the phone, and almost "run" the church. Early on, you would hear that the church was paying them $100 a week. Never did I assume this was a "real job", nor were the duties of the secretary, church custodian, and musician subject to taxes and personnel laws. The first time I heard about something like this becoming a problem was when I was in seminary and a church secretary retired and there was a great celebration praising her loyalty and service. A few weeks later, she went to apply for social security when she and the church learned that paperwork deductions, and forms should have been kept and sent to various government and social agencies were not reported properly. This woman had worked at the church for twenty-five years, and could not get "her" social security. You can imagine the confusion and discussion behind this problem.

Building an Effective Ministry Staff

As a Senior Pastor, I became actually aware of the severity of keeping good records of evaluation, commendation, and correction in a file for each church staff person. The day is over when a leader could walk into a church office and dismiss someone with no questions permitted, even in what is called "at will" state. This is when an employer can dismiss an employee at will. This does not stop the person from suing the supervisor or church. Sooner or later, church leaders will discovered that even forty year members who are dismissed or reprimanded would have no problem bringing a litigation against the ministry.

A church staff member can keep a pastor awake a night. But also a church staff member can also ease the load of pastoral ministry and concern. I am still learning, but I have some blood, sweat and tears. As the young folk say, "I have been there and have a T Shirt for it!" For a caring pastor, it is so hurtful when a staff member feels that the pastor and the church are their archenemy. They can spread discord and confusion among the membership. And yes, I have seen members and families join differing sides and even leave the church.

1

Ultimately, Dr. Mac and I, with almost 60 years of combined Church Administration and Leadership, wants you to know that the church must abide by the law of the land when it comes to hiring practices, promotions, job descriptions, annual compensations, and dismissals. Just as it takes time to build a church, it will take time to build a church staff that will meet the needs of the pastor and people, the pulpit and the pew. Another major misconception I had entering the ministry, was that everyone who called on the name of the Lord, loved the Lord. When hiring staff now, I must remind them differently.

Dr. William E. Flippin, Sr.
Senior Pastor
www.flippinlegacy.com

All Rise: Church Staffing
Building an Effective Ministry Staff

All Rise: Church Staffing

Building an Effective Ministry Staff

THE CHURCH STAFF

Help or Hindrance?

Chapter 1

The church staff should be viewed using the illustration of a rod. Just like the staff of a shepherd, the staff of the pastor serves various purposes for the ministry as a whole and for the pastor individually. There are three purposes for every rod/staff:

1. Supports the Pastor and aids the sheep

2. Disciplines the sheep

3. Has the potential to harm the sheep

Let us see how each of these purposes functions in the context of the church.

Support to the Pastor and Aid to the Sheep

This is the ideal relationship each member of your staff should have with the church and the ministry at large. No pastor can effectively operate a church without the support and help of others. It is imperative you place people

Building an Effective Ministry Staff

in positions where they can be effective. Take into consideration their effectiveness to the Pastor personally and the body of Christ at large. Every staff person has the potential to lead the church to high levels. Every great staff person should seek to support the vision of the Pastor in whatever area or department they have been called to serve. This is especially true if you are paid. It is important to support the Pastor, just as he/she would with a physical rod, be able to lean on their staff for support. When the Pastor feels weak, the staff should always be in a position to prop him/her on every leaning side. In the book of Exodus there is a great example of this in the relationship between Moses and his father-in-law Jethro. According to John Maxwell, the day Moses heeded to his father-in-law's advice was the day he became a leader.

The second ideal nature of the staff is to assist the Pastor in aiding the sheep. The staff of the church should be viewed as the arms and legs of the pastor. When the pastor is unavailable, the staff should be capable to step into this position with the same amount of passion and integrity as the pastor. As the aid to the sheep, it is the staffs responsibility to shelter the pastor from unnecessary work or stress. Having an effective staff, as aide to the sheep, permits the Pastor to focus on spiritual issues that will grow the church; not being tied up with day to day administration. It is important to note, it is impossible for a Pastor to give all of his/her attention to each member as well as manage administrative tasks and be effective. Thus having a strong staff of people surrounding the pastor will eliminate opportunities for pastor burn out.

Discipline to the Sheep

Choosing your staff and leaders should be a spiritual appointment. The resume, educational background, work experience and other criteria may influence the decision, however the decision should also be under-girded with prayer. As a Pastor, your staff should be trusted individuals. Not only are they trusted with daily duties and tasks, they should also be empowered to deal with persons in the church who may cause harm to the Body of Christ. All problems do not need to go to the Pastor. Again the purpose of the staff is to buffer unnecessary stress from the life of the pastor. An effective staff should have good people management skills. An effective staff should be able to execute best practices for disciplining in love. To the same degree an effective staff person should act in such a way that represents the best interest of the church and communicates the heart of the pastor.

Harm to the Sheep and the body at large.

Every staff will have its bad apples. There will be staff members who are lazy, non-team players, vindictive, selfish and unsupportive of the vision of the pastor and the church. It is imperative, as Dr. Samuel R. Chand teaches us, to discover staff persons who are ineffective and dismiss them. This can be hard for some churches and Pastors. In most churches, staff members are also church members and will have developed bonds and relationships with other members of the church. Some churches still chose to employ family and church members. Some staff members simply cannot keep up with the vision of the church because of age, competency or personal vices.

As a Pastor it is important to keep your staff relevant. Encourage your staff to continue their education and knowledge in the area they have been commissioned to serve. Empower them to take initiatives to explore their own leadership qualities. Always challenge them to become a better leader.

An ineffective staff member can become a liability to your church. Staff members will often have a greater visibility in the eyes of your members. Therefore, their actions will have a direct effect on how members view the ministry at large. A secretary who always has a bad attitude can harm the sheep. A minister of music who does not support the vision of the Pastor can harm the sheep. An administrator who has poor organizational skills can harm the sheep. Be sure your staff understands their role as it relates to building the kingdom of God and supporting the vision of the Pastor.

Building an Effective Ministry Staff

Building an Effective Ministry Staff

Staff Salaries: Public or Private Information?
Chapter 2

There has been much debate on whether or not church salaries should be disclosed to the public. Before we begin to look at this inquiry please keep under consideration that all "employee-employer" relationships should be handled with strict sensitivity and confidentiality. It is illegal to share this information. I do not recommend making this information public to the general public; however, I do believe members of the church who are financially contributing have a right to know how their tithes and offerings are being used. Salaries are an expenditure of the church. A member has the right to know how much the church spends on a new copy machine as well as what is paid out to persons for services rendered.

Because this is a sensitive issue, there should be a policy in place in order to protect the sensitivity of the information. To the same degree, this policy should be shared with the staff as well. I challenge you to take the following into consideration:

1. Church members have the right to review books and records of the church; as it relates to the business of the church. This should already be done in your church business sessions. Members have the right to review what comes in the church and what funds leave the church in the form of summary reports. On the contrary, church members DO NOT have the right to review specific payments to persons and DO NOT have the right to view other persons contribution information.

2. Church members DO NOT have the right to review personnel files regarding salaries and other benefits. This does not make the disclosure "illegal", should the church choose to disclose the information. However, there is no "legal" right stating a person has the right to review the information.

3. Your church can establish ways to make this information public by way of creating a policy for implementation. Staff

persons must be made aware of the policy decided on by the church. If they should have an issue with the policy they should be given the option to resign.

4. If your church does implement a policy, situation or guideline to make this information public, a system must be put in place to control the dissemination to members only. It should be understood that members only are welcome to opportunities where these type, sensitive matters, are disclosed. I would recommend position titles be listed in the church budget and the amount allocated for that position. Never list the person's name as this opens the opportunity for things to become personal and emotional.

5. Personnel profiles; including benefits, disciplinary actions, health records and other vital records should never be made available to members or non-members. The only persons who are privy to this information are designated leadership persons, chosen to handle this sensitive information.

6. Keep in mind, persons who are not paid large salaries may not want to have their salaries disclosed. Comparisons will kill a ministry.

Churches should remain sensitive to this issue and be guided by the spirit on how to make this information available. Each church has particular needs; so each church should develop their own policy and guidelines. All policies and guidelines should respect the privacy of the employee as well as fit the needs of the members who provide the funding for those positions. Larger churches may want to consider a pastoral staff policy and a non-pastoral staff policy. The levels of responsibilities are different; therefore the salaries will be different.

How are compensation profiles broken down?

1. Base salary
2. Retirement
3. Health Insurance
4. Housing Allowance
5. Life Insurance
6. Continuing Education

Building an Effective Ministry Staff

Staff often paid in the church

1. Senior Pastor

2. Assistant to the Pastor

3. Associate Pastors

4. Youth Pastor

5. Children's Pastor

6. Church Administrator

7. Pastor of Worship and Arts

8. Accountant/Book keeper

9. Custodian/ Property Maintenance

10. Part Time Employees

11. Contract Employees

12. Support Staff

When choosing to set salaries and packages for these positions ensure you do your research of what is fair and average in the church environment. Look at ministries in your area along with your church budget in order to determine what is fair and feasible *(excellent resources can be found on page 109).*

Building an Effective Ministry Staff

How to Manage an Effective Church Staff
Chapter 3

Human Resource Help

Whether you are a small ministry or a large congregation it is important to know and understand how your human resource strength supports the ministry of the church. Your Human Resources Department is like an engine. This can be handled by one person or a small group of persons. Your human resource persons are the first stop for new employees and your last stop for employed that are leaving. This is the area of your church where employee rules and regulations are created and implemented. Often when there are problems or issues with your staff your human resource persons will handle those issues, but only after their immediate supervisor or pastor could not resolve the matter.

Your human resource department is essential to develop and define the administration team. They, or this person, will set policy for all of the church's administrative

Building an Effective Ministry Staff

duties, ministry development activities, job descriptions, salary ranges, legal developments and other employment needs. The day to day operations of the church, and most supervision of staff, is to be done by the church administrator. All church administrators should be people of integrity who know how to balance the many facets that come along with people management in the church. To the same degree, the administrator and administrative staff must have a clear understanding of the vision of the ministry and their particular role in manifesting that vision.

The Church Administration Team's Goal

To ensure that administration in the ministry is handled using processes and procedures that line up with the mission, value, and vision of the ministry. The administration team seeks to effectively communicate and execute rules, regulations and policies to the staff. All administration teams should implement an open door policy.

The Role of the Administration Team/Person

1. Develop organized policies and procedures

2. Commit to making the policies and procedures relevant to governmental laws and safety laws

3. Maintain church records to the highest level of confidentiality

4. Attract, preserve, build up and inspire effective employees

5. Effectively communicate with Senior Pastor, Associate Pastors, Board and other church leaders about church functions.

6. Create compensation plans and packages for all employees (full time, part time and contracted)

7. Develop a system and policy in order to handle disciplinary actions in the event staff becomes ineffective or violates terms of employment

8. Dismiss ineffective staff.

Building an Effective Ministry Staff

Keeping your staff technologically savvy

There are many churches, and Pastors who still choose to operate without computers. With the advancement of culture changing daily it is important your church and staff are well aware of the technologies in place that will make their job easier. Encourage your staff to utilize computers, email, smart phones and websites that can advance their service. This will ultimately advance the church. A word to the wise would be to have a communication policy in place to keep from these technologies becoming abused.

Setting and Communicating standards with your staff

Each administrator and staff members should understand their working agreement and relationship with one another. Every administrator needs to effectively communicate and document what each staff member is expected to do in order to fulfill the job they have been hired to perform. Administration has the authority to empower staff to create their own mission, goals and plans; however a standard should be set regarding minimum expectations that will support the overall mission, goal and plans of the church.

28

Administration should ensure all employees receive documented information regarding policies, goals, expectations, benefits, etc. Church administrators have the right to determine which staff should attend leadership meetings and briefings. It is the administrator's responsibility to communicate the staff's requirements and input during these meetings. The administrator must ensure staff is competent on all materials presented to them regarding church policies and guidelines.

The Hiring Process

It is the administrations task to review internal and external candidates for employment at the church. There should be a hiring process at your church that is followed every time a paid position is to be filled.

Here are some things to consider before hiring:

1. The decision to hire has been approved based on need

2. In order to determine the position filled, ask your

ministry the following questions:

a. What is the need and why is it considered a need?

Building an Effective Ministry Staff

b. What duties will need to be fulfilled in this position?

c. Can these duties be accomplished using present staff?

d. How much training and competency will be required of this person?

e. Can the job be accomplished using volunteers?

Once you have decided to create and fill the position, the search to occupy the vacancy can be done using the following methods:

1. Church announcement
2. Newspaper ads
3. Pastoral Appeal
4. Resume and hiring search websites
5. Email marketing
6. Applicants can simply apply in the church office.

Effective Hiring Procedures

1. Ensure administration dates the application once it is received. If the applicant is a member of the ministry, pull the

individuals giving records to the church. This is not done in order to scrutinize the person because of their giving. This is done to determine if the member supports the church financially at all. Upon review of application, determine if the person meets the criteria needed to accomplish the specific job needs. If the person does not, file the application/resume for future review and send the applicant a letter stating their application was received.

2. Document when the application was given to the church administrator. He/she should forward the application to the personnel committee (HR). If the applicant is to work under a specific ministry leader or pastor, allow that person to review the application and resume as well. Because this person will be involved with the applicant on a daily basis, they may be better suited to note qualifications and experience.

3. The Human Resource Department is to set up a first interview with the applicant. Document when this interview is set up.

4. The Human Resource Department should obtain an interview form from the church file, or from the internet, that

will exemplify the work ethic and quality of the applicant. This interview is to establish the applicant that is best suited for the position. Salary, benefits and other specifics should not be discussed during this process.

5. If the Administrator, ministry leader and Pastor, decides to hire the applicant, a letter of recommendation is sent to the personnel committee. If these individuals do not want to hire the applicant, a simple "no" is indicated and documents are sent back to the personnel committee. The Church Administrator is responsible for writing a letter thanking the applicant for their interview.

6. Once the person has been selected for the position, a call is made by the Human Resource Department for a second interview with the Pastor. This interview will consist of more in-depth questions about the candidate's qualifications for employment. Within the interview, salary can be discussed. This interview should also include: insurance information, benefits, working hours, vacation days, sick days and other specifics. No promise of the position is made in this process.

7. After the second interview, it is confirmed between the Human Resource Department, church administrator, Pastor and ministry leader (if applicable) that they are in agreement to hire the potential candidate.

8. All interview and application material should be thoroughly discussed in order to confirm the correct candidate is selected.

9. The date of all approving the candidate should be documented.

10. If approved, the Church Administrator will draft a Job Offer Letter

11. If approved the letter should be mailed. However, most churches opt to call the candidate in for a third time in order to offer the position.

12. The applicant is then asked to accept or reject the offer; the date of decision is noted on the form.

13. If the applicant accepts the position, a start date is determined and documented.

14. The Church administrator is to communicate to all leaders the applicant has accepted the position and advise on the start date.

15. This process is highly effective. It keeps multiple leaders and persons in the loop about the selection process. This process ensures that qualified persons are selecting a qualified candidate.

Job/Position Description

During the orientation process, or in the Job Offer meeting, the new employee should be given a job description of their duties, responsibilities and expectations. A copy of this document is signed by the new employee and filed. A copy of the signed description is given to the new employee. The Job description is a detailed written statement that provides definition, goals, guidelines and stipulations the new employee will work within. The job description should also give the daily day-to-day responsibilities of the new employee.

Building an Effective Ministry Staff

Keep in mind the job description should document and describe the job and not person who is filling the position. All job descriptions should be as specific as possible. Stay away from generalized statements. Your job descriptions for all of your staff should be rather detailed and comprehensive. It should also include how the employee will be evaluated. It is recommended that all job descriptions within your church should be updated often in order to ensure the position remains up to date with society.

There are specific reasons a job description is important:

1. Essentially, job descriptions say who is responsible for what within the ministry. It also outlines how the specific job will relate to the other jobs and departments in the church. A well written job description leaves no room for ambiguity, can be used to settle disputes on performance and maximize communication among other staff members in your church.

2. Job descriptions are helpful as a reference to the Pastor, Church Leaders, Ministry Leaders and even members, as

to what is expected of the individual occupying the position. In order to prevent disorder, the job description helps others to look at the job that needs to be done and not the individual selected to do it.

3. A well-written job description will provide a standard for the employee's evaluation and salary stipulations. It can also help ministries determine if the employee is exempt or non-exempt.

4. The job description not only satisfies identifying a person who can fill the position. The job description is the tool used in order to determine if the employee's performance manifests the essential functions of the position.

Job descriptions should be written by the church administrator. The church administrator should seek counsel from the Senior Pastor, Human Resources Department and direct supervisor. There are many online sources that can provide you with sample job descriptions.

Legal Compliance

It is a good recommendation for the church to keep an attorney on retainer. Each year there are many employment legislations that are passed. It is important the church administrator becomes abreast in these new laws and policies. Church Administrators should be aware of seminars and forums discussing these issues. The church administrator should also be subscribed to legal publications and books regarding employment opportunities.

As a church you must abide by certain federal and state laws. Here are a few that hold great importance:

Fair Labor Standards Act (FLSA)

This particular act is also known as the wage/hour law. This law is enforced by the Wage and Hour division of the U.S. Department of Labor. There are 4 essential elements to this act. The elements include: minimum wage requirements, overtime requirements, child labor regulation and equal pay provisions.

Building an Effective Ministry Staff

Equal Pay Act

This act prohibits discrimination of wages or salary on the basis of sex or sexual orientation. In essence you cannot pay a man higher than a woman for doing the same equivalent job. If it is deemed the same qualifications, skills, responsibilities or descriptions are the same, both male and female should be paid the same amount.

Title VII of the Civil Rights Act of 1964

This act refers to discrimination based on race, ethnicity, religion, gender, or sexual orientation. Hiring, compensation, benefits and working conditions for all persons should be the same contingent on services offered. In the hiring process, none of the above mentioned should be criteria for hiring the individual.

Age Discrimination in Employment Act

This particular act only applies to employers who have 20 or more employees. This act prevents discrimination in the hiring process on individuals who are age 40 and over.

Family and Medical Leave Act

This act was designed for employers who have a total of 50 employees or more. The employee must be employed for 12 months and have worked a minimum of 1,250 hours within the previous 12 months to qualify. As a church you are required to offer your employee up to 12 work weeks of unpaid leave during any 12 month period for the following reasons:

1. Birth of a new born child to the employee

2. The placement of a child for adoption or foster care with an employee.

3. Caring for an immediate family member who has a serious health condition.

4. Self care for an employee who may have a serious health condition.

Building an Effective Ministry Staff

What every Administrator Needs to Know
Chapter 4

Orientations

It is important that all church administrators arrange time for new employees to be oriented to the church. Each church employee should be given a physical copy of the church handbook. It should be documented somewhere the new employee has received the book. Each new employee should have a clear understanding of what their job description entails along with their relationship to other ministry leaders and employees. It is recommended all church administrators utilize a checklist in order to confirm all materials and information about employment have been given to the new employee.

Training and Development

Training is essential but not always necessary in the ministry context. It is assumed the person who has applied for the specific position has the experience necessary to step directly into the role in which they were hired for. With regards to the employee's development, a well written job description will allow a person to see if the employee is measuring up to expectations. All church administrators should be available to help and assist employees as they make adjustments to the church environment.

Should there be any modification in your church manual or employee handbook, all current employees should be made aware of these changes. Be sure to include in your church budget opportunities for books, workshops, seminars, retreats and other work enhancing tools for your employees.

Grievance procedures

We do not live in a perfect world. Therefore, your church must have a method for handling grievances within your personnel. In most cases grievances can be settled by simple mediation. Keep in mind, persons often want their point of view to be heard and considered about an issue. We would recommend using the following three steps: 1. Employee should discuss the matter with their immediate supervisor. If the issue is not resolved, (2) an appointment should be made with the church administrator in order to discuss the matter. If the issue is still unresolved after this, (3) a time should be established to discuss the issue with the Senior Pastor. This procedure is modeled for us in Matthew 18. Reconciliation and the demonstration of Christ's love should always be the main objective.

How to become a better manager of people

Just as the church desires to be up to date on spiritual issues, the church should remain up to date on administrative issues. There are many sources provided that will help church administrators develop their administration skills. There are also new technologies that will help administrators maximize church productivity, time management and communication across the board. Administrators should be participating in seminars, webinars, book readings and consulting other churches in order to see what is working, and not working, in other ministries. Church Administrators should gain as much knowledge as possible! Church Administrators should also search for certification, or degreed, programs that will grow them as a leader. Personal growth equals church growth.

Building an Effective Ministry Staff

How to handle employee benefits?

It is the Church Administrators responsibility to administer non-cash compensation to church employees that qualify. These areas include, but are not limited to, insurance, retirement, paid time off, and other technologies that will assist the employee's performance.

Medical Insurance

All full-time, salaried church employees should be offered medical insurance to cover them and their family. Employees should apply for medical insurance per their church policy. This can be anywhere between 30-90 days. Many churches also provide prescription drug programs that help employees lower their prescription costs.

Dental & Vision Insurance

This is another benefit for employees which should be offered in the same way as medical insurance is offered. Some options will have the employer to pay half of the procedure done, leaving the other half for the employee. Be sure to shop around for what health plans work best for your ministry and your employees.

Life and Long Term Disability Insurance

As a ministry, life insurance should only be offered to specific employees. The life insurance policy should cover three times the annual salary of the person who is being covered. In some policies the church will pay half, leaving the other half for the employee to pay.

Retirement Plans

Many churches are classified as 501 (c)(3) nonprofit organizations. Because of this the option for employees to contribute into a 403(b)-retirement plan is possible. This particular plan is easy to set up and easy to join. Employees can opt into this plan at any time. It should be set so that the minimum contribution to this plan be $25 per pay period. This plan offers a convenient, regular savings program for employees.

Payroll and Time Keeping within the church

The needs of the church vary from week to week, however all paid employees should have a standard for the amount of time and hours they will put into the job. The church administrator, along with the finance persons should

Building an Effective Ministry Staff

coordinate how employees are paid. Salaries and wage break downs should be determined by the church administrator. There are many systems your church can use in order to process payroll.

Many banks will offer your church a Payroll system in order to help keep track of who is being paid and what they are being paid. Some sources, like ADP, are convenient in that they take care of your quarterly tax filings, produce W2s and keep files up to date with tax laws that could affect your payroll. If your ministry is still writing checks, by hand, from the general account, look into a technology grounded system that works for your ministry. Some companies also produce 1099 statements for contract employees on a yearly basis.

All church payroll summary statements should include:
- Payroll totals
- Hours and earnings analysis or both
- Analysis of
  o Federal income tax
  o SUI/SDI

Building an Effective Ministry Staff

- State Taxes
- City Taxes
- Miscellaneous information
- Taxable liability
- Federal deposit information
- Total pays
- Net pays, meaning total net amount of negotiable checks plus adjustments pays, but not including direct deposits
- Net cash, meaning total net amount of negotiable checks plus the total amount of direct deposits.

Staff Appreciation and Recognition

The Church Administrator is responsible for keeping the moral of the church staff high! For this reason it is their responsibility to plan and coordinate events and activities that will recognize the great work of the staff.

Employee Birthday Recognition

Each month our staff hosts a staff birthday lunch at the church. All persons who are celebrating their birthdays in that month will select a menu of their choice. A volunteer from the church will prepare the meal and serve the entire staff following the last staff meeting of the month.

Staff Appreciation

Every year our ministry has a staff appreciation Sunday. Members are encouraged to give a separate offering to show their love and appreciation for the staff. Whatever is collected is either divided among the staff or used in a corporate manner. Each ministry is petitioned to give their particular ministry leader special tokens of love.

Holiday Parties/Birthday Celebrations/ Employee Appreciations

During the holidays or a staff members birthday it is recommended the Church Administrator to provide an event for the staff. This can be done at a staff member's house or a local restaurant. Staff appreciations should be fun and enjoyable moments for the entire staff (i.e. Employment

Date Anniversary, Christmas Bonus, etc).

Healthy Living

A healthy employee can produce more than an unhealthy employee. Ensure your church staff is aware and encouraged to live a healthy lifestyle. It is recommended the Church Administrator to do one thing a year to promote good health. It is recommended that the Senior Pastor promote and create events that will support this livelihood as well. Insurance carriers may even provide credit to the church for hosting such activities.

All Rise: Church Staffing
Building an Effective Ministry Staff

Building an Effective Ministry Staff

MAXIMIZE THE MOMENTUM
OF YOUR MINISTRY
Chapter 5

The energy of your church will remain high as long as your church staff is empowered and encouraged. Located in your church staff code of conduct should be a sense of excitement, friendliness and warmth. Here are some examples of what your church should desire to display from its staff!

We work for the purpose of helping our members experience excellent ministry service

A. The staff should always be available for the service of others.

B. The staff should always display the love of Christ to embers and the community in a way that is unforgettable.

C. The staff understands their role is to make ministry easier for the Senior Pastor, leaders, other staff members and parishioners

Building an Effective Ministry Staff

The Staff should always be committed to creating a Christ centered environment

A. The staff is committed to always carry a welcoming attitude.

B. The staff does what it can to communicate in the most courteous ways to others.

C. The staff understands how their specific role impacts the ministry at large

D. The staff is committed to always present themselves in a neat, impeccable and professional manner.

E. The staff is committed to never speak negatively about others in the company of others.

A staff that manifests excellence

A. The staff is committed to treating all persons who come in contact with the ministry as an honored guest

B. The staff understands that a good or bad decision can have a tremendous impression in the long term representation of the church.

C. The staff is committed to calling persons by their name

D. The staff is committed to solving the problems of others as if it were a personal matter.

Building an Effective Ministry Staff

A Well Informed staff

A. Every staff member is committed to understand the general questions asked of members and others about the ministry and will always have an answer.

B. Staff is committed to personally hosting guests when they are on the campus of the ministry. The staff walks with guest and is committed not to pawn them off on another staff member until a matter is resolved or services are complete.

C. Staff members are committed to identifying persons who can answer/solve problems when they arrive. No staff member will pass guest on to other unqualified persons to handle the problem.

Every staff member knows their role in creating an excellent ministry.

A. Each staff member will seek to achieve the vision of the church

B. Each staff member will keep their areas of service and work clean and neat.

C. Staff will document instances where members were served in an outstanding manner

D. Every team member is empowered to resolve problems in the event of member dissatisfaction. The ultimate goal of the team member is to ensure the problem does not happen again.

Staff Members will Create an Environment pleasing to God

A. Team members commit to ensuring their area of work is safe.

B. Team members will communicate to the church administrator all hazardous situations and injuries

C. Team members will be good stewards of the resources they have been entrusted with and will protect the assets of the church.

Team Work Makes the Dream Work

A. Members will work to support other team members and leaders throughout the church.

B. Team members commit to friendly and formal environment

C. Team members vow to take their jobs seriously, but not themselves

Building an Effective Ministry Staff

D. Team members commit to be flexible and to keep their role and actions fun and energetic

E. Team member commits to open communication and to stay away from malicious attitudes.

A staff that handles personal problems with faith

A. Team members will keep spiritual focus in all aspects of their life

B. Team members know the church is available to assist them in their time of personal needs.

C. Team members know how to not allow personal manners effect their ability to uphold the church's code of conduct.

Keenly be aware of when the applicant has been at other jobs or churches. It is important to call their previous employer in order to ask critical questions regarding the person's character. Other things to consider asking might also include looking at how a person handles criticism and what are the applicant's educational goals. Also understand that if a person had a bad attitude or work ethic in the secular world,

Building an Effective Ministry Staff

do not expect things to be different in the church world.

Employee Staffing and Compensation
Chapter 6

Staffing Your Church

Church staff, just as any other company, business or organization, must function and operate in a professional and business like manner. The church office should be the brain and nerve center of the church. Members should not have the freedom to lounge or hang around the office with small talk. Visitors to the office should be warmly greeted and readily directed or assisted with their needs. Church officials should hold in high regard and maintain good work ethics and professionalism.

Job Descriptions

A detailed job description should be prepared for each employee. Job descriptions spell out the duties and responsibilities for each position and who the employee is accountable to. Job descriptions are valuable tools in evaluating an employee's job performance over time. You cannot in fairness hold an employee accountable for good job performance when their job has not been clearly defined.

Building an Effective Ministry Staff

Job Qualification Statements

These statements give the candidate a summary of the job descriptions, specify qualifications, or skills required, previous experience desired or required, educational requirements, travel requirements, and salary range.

Minimum Staffing

A beginning church usually cannot afford to hire full time employees. Often, the pastor has another full time job and serves the church on a part time basis. When a church is in position to hire employees, I would recommend these minimum positions to start with, whether full-time, part-time, or voluntary:

1) Pastor,
2) Secretary, and
3) Bookkeeper
4) Music Staff
5) Custodian/ Maintenance

The secretary initially will serve both the pastor and the church. As the church grows and ministries develop, the church should seriously consider hiring more clerical help (full or part time).

A bookkeeper is the key to keeping track of income

Building an Effective Ministry Staff

and expenses and recording contributions. The secretary should not be expected to perform these duties. Initially, the bookkeeper can be a part time employee, working only two or three days a week.

Other Staffing Positions

As your church grows, (and I'm sure it will) and more and more in reach and outreach ministries develop, you will definitely need to hire additional qualified employees. The pastor cannot do all of the work of the ministry by his/her self. With proper planning and budgeting, as the need for additional employees materializes, the funds will be available. Other staff positions may be, but are not limited to:

- Custodian/ Maintenance
- Receptionist
- Business Manager
- Counselor
- Pastoral Care Minister
- Musicians
- Youth and Children's Ministers
- Minister of Music & Arts
- Christian Education Director

- Comptroller
- Special Events Coordinator

Generally speaking, the pastor should handle the hiring and discharging of the employees. Additionally, the pastor should have the freedom and flexibility to choose his or her own staff. After all, the buck stops at his or her desk. Boards should not tie the pastor's hand in this matter.

Compensating Your Employees

What's a fair compensation? It's true that churches cannot compete with the public and private sector. Churches and other nonprofit organizations must raise their funds because they are dependant upon free will gifts or contributions. Having said that, churches should be fair in their employee compensation. Remember, these people have families, responsibilities, needs, wants, and desires like anyone else.

Determining Fair Compensation

This is not hard to do. Remember that old saying, "Compare apples to apples." Here's how!

Building an Effective Ministry Staff

Call other churches in your area of a comparable size, income, and if possible domination and see if they will share with you their salary range for certain positions.

Repeat the same procedure by contacting churches in the same region of the country in which you reside. Note: You would only call those churches you have a relationship with. Churches that you do not have a relationship with, write a letter to the pastor explaining you are bringing your church salary ranges in line with other churches in your region and you would appreciate his help by sharing information with you. If he/she responds, you should send the pastor a "thank you" letter.

All of the above work has already been done for you. Several church administration organizations publish periodic salary surveys. They are:

- NACBA -National Association of Church Business Administration
- CMA – Christian Management Association

Building an Effective Ministry Staff

Sometimes, there is a nominal cost for these salary surveys but they are well worth the investment and should be a part of your library. Most are free of charge on their website.

Salary Ranges

Again, with proper planning and budgeting, an established church should develop and maintain salary ranges for all employees. Salary ranges are a morale booster. Employee should have no doubt when their next raise should be. Every year on their anniversary date (hire date) for the next 5-7 years they know and can expect to receive an annual pay

Salary Ranges help boost employee morale

increase. For smaller churches that may not be able to have established salary ranges, a definite policy to at least give some form or a cost of living adjustment would be in order.

Do Not Promise: As a church and ministry grows so does the expenses. Many staff members have become bitter and left the church because this statement was made.

Fringe Benefits

In addition to salary, you should consider the following fringe benefits:

62

Workman's Compensation Insurance – Is required by law in most states for churches. It covers work related injured and loss. Most healthcare providers require you to have workman's compensation before they will issue coverage

Health Insurance Coverage- **group** health coverage should be offered to your employees. Cost for coverage is usually shared by employer and employees on a percentage scale. Ex. 60/40% or 50/50%. Another method may be that the church pays the employees premium and the employee pays for any dependant coverage.

Your health insurance coverage may include the following benefits for a nominal fee:

- Life Insurance
- Dental Coverage
- Optical Coverage
- Disability Coverage

Housing Allowance

For qualified ministers only – The Internal Revenue Code grants a special privilege to qualified ministers, called a

> You may reduce your pastor's income tax liability if they qualify for a housing allowance

parsonage exclusion. Or better known as a housing allowance. The housing allowance permits the following to qualified ministers, subject to certain restrictions.

1. If a minister has a home (parsonage) provided by the church as part of his/her salary plan, the minister pays no income tax on the rental value of the home.

2. If a home is not provided but the minister receives a housing allowance from the church for housing expanses, he/she pays no tax on the allowance

3. Restrictions for receiving this privilege according to

Section 107 of the Internal Revenue Code are:

a. Must be qualified minister of the gospel as defined by the IRS

b. The housing exclusion must be by official designation, (in writing by the church).

c. The housing exclusion must be designated by official action prior to payment

d. The housing exclusion is to be used by the minister to rent or provide a home

Mileage Reimbursement

If the church expects an employee to use their personal vehicle for church business and errands, the church should at least be willing to reimburse the employee for mileage. The church must have a system by which mileage is logged and employees are reimbursed at the rate established by the IRS.

Paid Holidays

The church should have an established written policy on paid holidays observed by the church. At minimum, paid holidays should include the following:

- New Years Eve & New Years Day
- Dr. Martin Luther King's Birthday

- Good Friday (if no special services are planned)
- Memorial Day
- July 4th
- Labor Day
- Thanksgiving Day
- Christmas Eve & Christmas Day

Paid Sick Leave

The church should have established written policy on paid sick leave for employees. To be fair and competitive, I would recommend investigating other churches in your vicinity about their sick leave policy. Consider whether sick leave will include funerals, maternity leave, and short trips to the doctor or dentist.

Family and Medical Leave (FMLA)

The FMLA of 1993 requires certain employers to provide up to twelve weeks of unpaid leave to eligible employees. This law applies to organizations with 50 or more employees. Employees are eligible for this leave for the birth of a child and certain other reasons provided they have been employed at least 12 months and worked at least

1250 hours. However, churches with less than 50 employees (the majority) should seriously consider adopting this policy.

Birthday Leave

A good morale booster would be a written policy that employees receive their birthday off with pay. The time off will pay great dividends in a loyal and appreciative employee.

Building an Effective Ministry Staff

Insuring Your Church, Employees & Church Property
Chapter 7

Your church should be fully insured and your property coverage should provide for comprehensive and general liability insurance. Your general

Be sure your church is properly insured

insurance package should include, but not be limited to the following:

Fire loss/damage

Replacement cost new

Flooding

Earthquakes

Sprinkler System leaks

Musical instruments

Employee dishonesty

Employee owned vehicles

Sexual Harassment/abuse

Personal computers

Windstorm, hail

Explosions, riots

Aircraft

Water damage

P.A. system

Church contents

Theft, burglary

Charter trips

Workman's Compensation

Office copier(s)

Building an Effective Ministry Staff

The limits of coverage for your church should be based on the value of your property as determined by a fair market appraisal and not what you paid for it.

Ask your insurance agent about "Umbrella Liability Insurance" coverage to increase your liability limits.

Vehicle Insurance

Church-owned and operated vehicles are to be totally insured. This should include liability, comprehensive, and medical coverage on church owned automobiles, trucks, vans, and buses. Limits of liability should be based on vehicle usage. For instance, if you have a church operated van to transport children to your child care center or transport seniors to church services, your liability limit should be higher than minimum state limits. Also, your coverage should include "loss of use" and "vehicle rental.

Loss of Use covers the church if a church vehicle is in an accident and out of commission. Your insurance company will rent the church a suitable vehicle until repairs

Building an Effective Ministry Staff

are made. This is true if the church is at fault, it will also rent the other party a vehicle.

Most vehicle coverage will allow the church to rent a vehicle, without having to accept the rental car company's higher insurance coverage.

Lastly, be sure to include uninsured motorist coverage to insure church owned vehicles in the event of an accident involving someone without insurance protection. Your church insurance package should also cover employees and church volunteers if they have been authorized to use their personal vehicles for church's business.

Employee Insurance

A beginning church may not be able to afford group insurance for its employees, but it should be a high priority as funds become available. You will find it difficult to attract and retain good employees without offering this benefit. People can only volunteer for so long.

Building an Effective Ministry Staff

Group Hospitalization Insurance

Sometimes called medical insurance or health insurance, hospitalization insurance falls into three basic categories, namely HMO, PPO, and Indemnity.

An HMO or Health Maintenance Organization is a prepaid plan where medical care is provided by a health maintenance organization. The advantage of an HMO is once you have paid your monthly premium and a small co-payment, there are no additional out-of-pocket expenses. The main disadvantage is that you must use their pre-approved physicians and sometimes their facilities.

A PPO or Preferred Provider Organization is where medical care is provided by a network of hospitals and physicians at reduced or discounted rates.

Indemnity insurance is perhaps the most familiar form of health insurance. The insured pays a monthly premium and there is a required deductible, usually 80/20. The insured pays the first 20% of medical bills up to a limit and

All Rise: Church Staffing

once the limits are reached, the insurance company pays 100% coverage. There are usually co-insurance provisions.

Group Life Insurance

Employees can be provided minimum life insurance for very reasonable rates. The first $50,000 of coverage is tax-free. A $10,000 or $15,000 life insurance coverage for employees is common. Dependants can be included at very reasonable rates also (usually from about $2,000 to $2,500 of coverage.) *See chapter 4

Disability Dental, Optical

This coverage can be a part of your health insurance packet, with all or part provided by your health insurance carrier. There are dental insurance providers that work like an HMO or PPO. There is a network of pre-approved dentists from which you choose. For a monthly premium, you receive dental care at a reduced or discounted rate. Usually, routine care like x-rays, biannual cleanings and fillings is available at no additional charge.

Building an Effective Ministry Staff

Optical care is usually provided through a vision center with eye exams provided at reduced rates as well as prescription lenses, contacts, and frames.

Board of Directors and Officers Liability Insurance

The church should provide protection for its pastor, directors, trustees, officers, administrators, etc. against certain liabilities, which may incur while they perform their official duties on behalf of the church. These persons provide a valuable service to the church often without compensation and in the event of legal action; their attorney fees will be paid. Many states have laws protecting persons who serve as volunteers on boards for non-profit organizations, churches included. Be sure to inquire with your insurance agents.

Key Person Insurance

In most churches, the pastor has the main responsibility of raising church funds. Raising the church's budget rests on his/her shoulders and if the pastor were suddenly called home the church would undoubtedly experience financial shortfalls. It also takes time, probably several months, to secure another pastor. You may want to seriously consider "Key Man" coverage for the pastor in the event of an untimely death.

Building an Effective Ministry Staff

Communications and Public Relations (PR) Chapter 8

First impressions are usually lasting impressions. The church is a city that sits upon a hill, and it cannot be hid. All eyes are on the church to be that place of hope, refuge, and salvation, which Christ intended it to be. The perception that people receive when they visit or call your church will make a lasting impression that will either draw them to or drive them from you. Careful thought and planning should be given to how your church will be presented or communicated to the public.

Mission and Vision Statement

Church mission and vision statements are discussed in our book, "Managing with Ministry Excellence". Remember that your mission statement is the biblical reason your church exists, and your vision statement tells how you expect to work out your mission statement in your church or ministry. As you stay focused on your mission and vision for ministry, you will find it easy to consistently and effectively make those lasting and positive first impressions about your church.

Your mission and vision statements should be visible for all to see – in the vestibule, office, lobby, board or conference rooms, Sunday School classrooms, anywhere groups gather. As people see and read them over and over again, they will become embedded in their subconscious mind. Before long, people will be able to communicate the mission and vision of their church without hesitation and with conviction. Include your mission statement on your church stationary, Sunday bulletins, newsletters, Internet website, and other publications. Keep it before your people, both young and old. You are planting seeds that, over time, will grow and mature into faithful and committed members of your church and the body of Christ.

Ushers and Greeters

Ushers and greeters are the initial public relations staff of your church. Many undecided persons have decided

Building an Effective Ministry Staff

to join churches because of the warmth, love and care they received from ushers or greeters when they first entered the vestibule. In contrast, many persons were turned away and never looked back because they were met by a cold, insensitive, and uncaring usher or greeter. Can you imagine the negative press your church will receive? It is said in advertising that the best form of advertising is word of mouth.

The Psalmist said, "I had rather be a doorkeeper in the house of my God, than to dwell in the tents of wickedness." (Psalms 84:10). Ushers, especially, are the foot soldiers of the church. They are on the front line to receive abuse, frustrations, stubbornness, and outright rebellion from members and visitors. The must enforce the policies of the pastor for the worship services and help to maintain order and discipline. They serve the congregation by distributing literature, passing the offering tray (in some churches), and helping in whatever way they are called upon. Ushers must do all this with both a smile and a positive attitude. It is little wonder that ushers need to be called by God.

Visitor's Information Packet

A Visitor's Information Packet is a valuable communication and public relations tool for your church or ministry. Every first-time visitor should receive this information. This packet will educate, inform, and provide insight about your church ministry.

We live in the information age where many people are thirsty for information to help them finalize their decisions. Your visitor information packet should include the following items:

- Welcome Letter from the Pastor
- Foundational statements
- Visitor's information card (this card should be completed and returned during the worship service)
- List of ministries you offer
- Worship opportunities
- Response or comment card
- Envelope (You may elect to use a "Visitor's Offering" envelope to track visitors.)

Visitors Letter

A Letter should be sent to all first-time visitors from the Pastor. This is a "Thank You" letter to express appreciation for their visit to your church. This letter should be received by the visitor prior to the next Sunday. As a personal touch in the letter, you could include the names of other family members who accompanied them, if the names are available. You may also include a small gift such as a bookmark, church newsletter, cassette tape, informational pamphlet, or daily devotional book. Lastly, if possible, the Pastor should personally sign the letter.

Telephone Etiquette

Like ushers and greeters, the person(s) answering the telephone can either turn people on or off about your church. Perhaps 99% of the time, the church secretary or receptionist will answer the telephone. A proper business atmosphere should be maintained at all times. The secretary or receptionist should be knowledgeable about the church's organization so that calls are directed to the proper person

Building an Effective Ministry Staff

This person should also be able to answer routine inquiries about worship and office hours, directions to the church, and general information about the church's ministries. The secretary/receptionist should also know if a staff member is out of the office and their expected time of arrival or return.

Some characteristics of a professional secretary/receptionist are:

- Good diction and pronunciation

- Cordial, polite, and even tempered

- Helpful and courteous to callers and visitors

- General knowledge of various church ministries

- Knowledgeable of staff member responsibilities and functions

- Able to master your telephone system

- Able to take clear, precise, and often detailed messages

Telephone Answering System

In order to communicate with your congregation and the general public after office hours, you will need a telephone answering system or an answering service. In either case, messages should be retrieved as soon as reasonable and followed up immediately. Most after hour calls may be visitors calling about your worship hours and directions to your church. In your opening greeting, you could include information which will alleviate the caller's need to leave a message. Your opening greetings should be clear, precise, and brief. I recommend that you use a pleasant and welcoming voice to record your greeting.

Church Stationary

A good public relations tool for your church is the design and selection of your stationary. Your letterhead and stationary reflect the image or brand of your church. Well-designed, crisp, and quality stationary gives the impression of a well-managed, first-class church. Likewise, mediocre or

Building an Effective Ministry Staff

poor stationary will give the opposite impression. Your stationary represents you wherever it goes.

Be sure to select a good quality paper for your outgoing business-related correspondence. Choose a soft-colored paper and compatible ink for your letterhead, envelopes, and business cards to perhaps match your church's color.

I recommend that only the pastor's name be printed on your stationary. The reason for this is that in most churches, the pastor is the only constant and you would not have to print new stationary each time new officers or department heads change. I also recommend that you include your mission statement on your stationary.

Other Communication and PR Tools

Church bulletins – The church bulletin provides a means for the church to communicate with the congregation without having to make every announcement during the worship service. Members and friends can be informed of major upcoming church events, sick and shut-in members,

Building an Effective Ministry Staff

birthdays, group meetings, community events and much more.

Calendar of Events – This is an excellent tool to keep members aware of all church activities on an annual basis. An annual church calendar containing all church, auxiliary, and departmental events can be published at a reasonable cost for every member to have in their home. Pictures of the month, which highlight church activities along with an applicable scripture verse, could be an excellent fundraiser and added public relations tool for your church

Bulletin Board – A bulletin board could be located in an area where member congregate to post useful information. In addition members could post information for the other members regarding available jobs, business opportunities, homes and cars for sale, and other useful information.

Church Business Directory- The church could publish a directory of all members who own or operate businesses or provide professional services. The members would have this business directory and would be encouraged by the pastor to patronize these persons. Perhaps, saving coupons or discounts could be offered and members would tithe back to the church on their profits. The directory could also be located in the church office as a referral tool to advise persons who may be inquiring about a particular desired business or service

Leadership Conferences – The pastor should meet with the leaders monthly or quarterly to maintain open communication and dialogue. This is a golden opportunity for the pastor to effectively communicate, inform, and educate leaders about all facets of the ministry. This is also the time for the pastor to receive feedback from leaders, clarify areas of misunderstanding, resolve conflicts, nip things in the bud, and praise good performance.

Church Business Meetings – **The** pastor should meet with the entire congregation periodically in a non-worship setting with no offering being raised. The format

Building an Effective Ministry Staff

would be more like a "fireside chat" to brief the congregation on past accomplishments, failures, upcoming goals, and objectives. This should be a "family" meeting and not a "bear" meeting. Members should be allowed to ask questions and give feedback. Openness communicates that everyone is on the same page and there is nothing to hide.

Media – The radio, television, and newspaper can provide a valuable service of communicating to the public about events and activities of your church. Radio and television stations provide public service announcements (PSA's) at no cost. For major functions or events, you may elect to produce a radio or television announcement (spot) or purchase advertising in your local newspaper. If you engage in something of importance to the community, the media will often provide press coverage.

Internet – Perhaps, you have heard the terms, information superhighway, cyberspace, or Internet. They all are all one in the same. The church must accept the fact that the Internet is here to stay. The personal computer (PC) is

Building an Effective Ministry Staff

probably the technological marvel of this century. At the turn of the 20th century, the major source of information and mass communication was the printed page. Now, less than one hundred years later and from the comfort of your own home, you can click on your PC and the world is virtually at your fingertips.

More and more churches are taking advantage of this new technology. You can have your own church web site designed to communicate the mission and vision of your church People all around the world can "click on your website via the Internet to learn and receive information about your church or ministry. A few features you can provide are:

- A picture and message from the pastor (either text or audio)
- Video scenes of your church
- Information about your church and ministries
- Church newsletter

Building an Effective Ministry Staff

- How to order media, books and other items on the internet
- Calendar of upcoming events

The sky is limitless with the internet. If you have not moved into the computer age, you need to do so now and make it one of your number one public relation priorities. If you have computers in your office, its time to "hook up" with the internet, like yesterday.

Building an Effective Ministry Staff

THE ESSENTIALS
Chapter 9

CHURCH INVENTORY

The church should maintain a complete and detailed inventory of all its equipment and permanent contents. This will prove to be invaluable in the event of theft or loss by fire, water damage, or some natural disaster should occur. Also, if the church is "for sale", an inventory of all church equipment and contents aid in determining a fair selling price. Most professional church audits require this information.

The church should begin by inventorying church equipment and contents in a systematic way. A member with some accounting background could chair a special committee to inventory the church. The committee might function like this:

1. The pastor or trustee board could appoint an inventory committee and a chairperson.

Building an Effective Ministry Staff

2. Inventory forms are provided to the committee or the committee could devise their own forms.

3. The pastor or trustee board should give the committee a deadline to complete their task and charge them with submitting a complete and detailed report.

4. Depending on the size of the church, the committee should be divided into small groups to inventory various church departments (i.e. Church office, music dept., Christian education, youth dept., audio ministry, kitchen and fellowship hall, bookstore etc).

5. The church and its leaders should be amply informed that a special committee has been appointed to inventory the church within a specified time and their cooperation is needed.

6. The chairperson of the committee should appoint one or two persons to meet with the church finance office to review past invoices, bills of sales, contracts or receipts to obtain dates, model numbers, serial numbers, brands, and cost of items acquired.

7. Committee members should contact individual department and auxiliary leaders to coordinate a date and time to inventory their equipment and contents with their

assistance.

8. The chairperson should meet with committee members weekly for follow-up reports and problem solving. Any major problem should be referred to the pastor or board to resolve.

9. The inventory committee should categorize its report to show the location in the church of equipment and contents (i.e., sanctuary, library, office 204, etc.)

There is a church inventory software package available for this purpose. Whenever the church acquires additional equipment or contents, they should be immediately added to the inventory list before being placed in service (there may be a few exceptions to this rule, say a new boiler). Also, any equipment or contents being retired should be noted on the master inventory file. The trustee board of the church should be accountable for maintaining church inventory records.

TIME MANAGEMENT

The key to effective church administration and management is being able to manage one's time by practicing time management principles. Recognize the fact that there is a set amount of time in each day and you will never be able to accomplish all you think you need to in a single eight hour work day. Here are some time management techniques you can begin to incorporate in your life.

Plan Ahead

You've heard the saying, "Plan your work and work your plan." Planning will help you to stay on task to accomplish daily objectives.

Use Daily Planners or To Do Lists

These are written tasks and projects you plan to accomplish on a daily basis. Personally, I would recommend using the Day Timers ® time management systems. You can keep track of tasks, phone calls, appointments, and daily expenses.

Prioritize Tasks

Use A, B, C codes to prioritize your tasks or projects in your daily planner or To Do List. A's are your high priority items, B's are your important items, and C's are your less important tasks. (Tasks you can delegate)

When to Prioritize Tasks

You should take about 15-20 minutes at the end of the day to reflect and review what you have accomplished that day. Then those tasks or projects you did not complete will be moved forward to the next day, along with any new tasks and projects. You then re-prioritize the task for the next day so that when you arrive to work the next morning you are ready to start.

Procrastination

Avoid putting off for tomorrow what you can do today. Procrastination is a time waster. Remember to stay on task, plan your work, and work your plan.

Other Time Wasters

* Long telephone conversations

*Open door policy

*Unexpected visitors

*Poor planning

*Indecision

*Unnecessary meetings

Delegate- Don't do what someone else can do better. Delegate or assign tasks to them to complete. Follow-up and periodic reporting is important.

Provide Training- Training should precede the permanent assignment of all tasks. Do not take it for granted that people know how to carry out their assignment. Be sure to go over their job description with them in detail. Even a small amount of training will reap significant benefits.

Allow People to Fail- *Mistakes* will happen but conscientious people will learn from their mistakes. Start by giving them small or non-important jobs to do at first, so if they make a mistake it is not a serious crisis. Explain to them in a helpful and caring way about their mistake. Help them grow- you are grooming valuable team members.

Praise Good Work- *Everyone* likes to know they are needed and appreciated. Praise Good work, initiative, creativity, and going beyond the call of duty. You will find that people will not be working just for a paycheck, but because they love their work.

Building an Effective Ministry Staff

RECOMMENDED CHURCH POLICIES

Chapter 10

Policy statements are vital to the effective operation and management of your church. Policy statements should be in writing and available for leaders and members alike. They should be adopted by the governing board or voted on by the church body, depending on your church bylaws.

Some recommended church policies are listed below:

1. *Benevolent Assistant-* state the condition on which the church will assist the benevolent needs of members and non-members.

2. *Check Cashing-* The church should have a written "NO CHECK CASHING" policy.
   Unfortunately, some persons have written a check to the church desiring the church cash the check. During tax time, they take the cancelled check and claim it as a contribution.

3. *Contribution Statements-* state the procedure for a member or visitor to receive their individual contribution statement from the financial secretary at any given time and an annual contribution statement for income tax purposes.

4. *Contributions Envelopes-* State the church's policy of maintaining accurate records of member contributions by using an envelope system

5. *Corporate Credit Cards-* State rules and conditions for who is authorized to use the church credit card. Also define limitations, areas of usage, reporting procedures, personal use, and reimbursement

6. *Counseling-* State the areas of counseling the church will provide, any waiver form to be signed, confidentiality clauses, and who is authorized to counsel.

7. *Equipment Loan Policy-* Outline procedures for loaning and returning church property or equipment to members and other church or non-profit organizations (schools, community groups, etc.)

8. *Express Mailing-* Outline procedures of what constitutes express mailing, who can authorize overnight mailing, and whether a package should go standard, priority, or same day. Determine whether the U. S. Postal Service or other carriers should be used.

9. *Financial Review of Records-* *Outline* who and when the financial records can be reviewed. Check state laws if you are an incorporated church.

10. *Floral-* State the condition and rules for when flowers, floral sprays, potted plants, and cards are to be sent to members or a member's relatives.

11. *Funerals-* State the condition for use of the church by members, non-members, church family members who are non-members, and procedures for funeral services and feeding the family.

12. *Group Fundraising-* Outline procedures for when department and auxiliaries can contract with fundraising companies to raise needed funds. State who can sign contracts on behalf of the church.

13. Loan to Members – state the Board's written policy that the church does not loan money. The church's bylaws should allow only for benevolent assistance to members and non-members.

14. Petty Cash – outline procedures and limits for using petty cash funds.

Building an Effective Ministry Staff

15. Reimbursement Plan – outline procedures for how employees or members can be reimbursed for using personal funds for an approved church expense.

16. Retuned checks – outline procedures for collecting on retuned checks and the fees to be assessed.

17. Sexual Abuse/Harassment – outline the procedure for screening employees and volunteers to avoid sexual abuse/harassment problems and what action the church will take if it determined that there is a problem. Annual training must be required of church staff and leaders. The church should be protected with sexual harassment/abuse insurance coverage.

18. Uniform Purchases – outline under what conditions, if any, the church will assist with the purchase of robes and uniforms for the pastor, choir members, kitchen workers, ushers, and others. Also, how these robes or uniforms will be stored and cleaned.

19. Use of Church Fellowship Hall – outline procedures for renting or leasing the church facility by members, non-members, other groups or individuals and the related fees.

20. Use of Office Equipment – outlines procedures for allowing members to use church equipment such as copiers, fax, computer, typewriter, and audio duplication equipment. The policy should also state under what conditions the equipment can be used and if there are any related costs.

21. Weddings – state the rules for decorating the church, rehearsal times, wedding procedures, any allowance for secular songs, moving church furniture, reception in fellowship hall and the applicable fees.

RECOMMENDED CHURCH FORMS

When properly used, forms allow for ease of communication. They ensure that all the information needed to make a good decision is readily at one's fingertip. Forms provide uniformity of information and make for easy filing and retrieval.

Listed below are a few recommended forms that will increase the efficiency of your ministry. (See Appendix for samples)

103

Building an Effective Ministry Staff

1. Accident/injury form
2. Announcement request
3. Benevolent Assistance
4. Church Activity request
5. Death of member or loved one
6. Equipment loan
7. Floral Log
8. Leader's performance evaluation
9. Long distance log
10. Member illness
11. Overnight mailing
12. Requisition Request
13. Vehicle Accident Report
14. Vehicle Maintenance Report
15. Vehicle Mileage Log

Appendix

SAMPLE JOB DESCRIPTIONS

Minister of Music

The Minister of Music shall serve as the Chief Administrator of the Music Department and shall develop and coordinate a spiritually effective and harmonious program of music for our local church assembly. The Minister of Music shall provide spiritual leadership and maintain exemplary conduct in attitude and in deed and shall be accountable to the Pastor and shall serve under the supervision of the Associate Minister of Worship

Duties and Responsibilities

1. Shall directly supervise all choir directors. Shall assist choir directors as needed in the choice and arrangements of church music in keeping with the ministry or the Pastor and Church

2. Shall assist all choir directors and musicians as needed in the selection of and rendering of appropriate music for worship services.

3. Shall work directly with all choir directors in scheduling and coordinating all rehearsals for individual or combined choirs.

4. Shall work directly with all choir directors in establishing policies, rules, dues, and fees for the effective and efficient operation of the choir.

5. Shall be responsible for penalizing all personality and attitude problems, misunderstandings, and general concerns that may arise.

6. Shall approve of all engagements, with Pastoral consent of choir visitation and participation in other worship services.

7. Shall coordinate fund raising efforts to support the expansion of the music ministries and shall be responsible for maintaining all musical instruments and any repairs needed to keep them in good operating condition

8. Shall be a positive supporter of the ministry and program of the church and Pastor

9. Shall work with the Director of Training and Recruiting and the Advisory Board of the Music Department to promote and provide for a harmonious atmosphere so that all choirs may function effectively.

10. Shall attend the monthly Leadership Conference and submit a monthly progress report to the Pastor.

Church School Superintendent

The Church school superintendent shall be accountable to the Director of Christian Education and shall develop and coordinate an effective program of Bible study and Christian Education, which supports and operates with our Pastor's vision.

Duties and Responsibilities

1. Shall coordinate a departmentalized Church School which shall teach students the Word of God and shall inspire and motivate them to be effective witnesses for Christ.

2. Shall educate and supervise a staff of Spirit -filled teachers, dedicated to the ministry of teaching and Christian evangelism.

3. Shall conduct regular teacher's meetings, training sessions, workshops, seminars as necessary to perfect the overall Church School Department.

4. Shall oversee the "New Members Ministry" of our church. A program designated to orientate new members to this ministry.

5. Shall sponsor field trip, programs, workshops, and other activities that will enhance the overall Church School program.

5. Shall perform any other related projects as deemed necessary by the Pastor

6 Shall attend the monthly leadership conference and submit a monthly progress report to the Pastor.

SAMPLE CHURCH PERSONELL POLICY

Christ Church

Name of Pastor

Street Address City,

State, Zip Code Phone

and Fax Numbers

Website Address

COVER PAGE

Employee Handbook

EMPLOYEE VALUES

BELIEVING THESE QUALITIES TO BE PLEASING TO OUR HEAVENLY FATHER, WE PLEDGE HONESTY, INTEGRITY, AND HONOR. WE DELIGHT ALL WITH WHOM WE INTERACT BY OUR ACTIONS AND OUR COMMITMENT TO EXCELLENCE AT CHRIST CHURCH.

All Rise: Church Staffing
Building an Effective Ministry Staff

TABLE OF CONTENTS

Benefits

INTRODUCTION

Christ Church forms a special kind of work environment. We are a church with clearly defined Mission and Vision Statements and that is to serve the people. We are a church with special kinds of people and we share a commitment to Jesus Christ. We desire to live by His principles and to share in the life of our church.

Christ Church is concern about its employees. We want their salaries to be equitable, their benefits to be generous, and their working conditions to be wholesome. Because of these concerns, we have approved a personnel policy manual. We hope this manual will be helpful to you as you work here.

As an employee, there are ways in which you can help create a good work environment. If you see something that can be improved, please share your ideas with your supervisor. If you do not understand something in the manual, the Church Administrator or members of the Personnel Committee will be glad to answer any questions you might have. If you think you have not been treated fairly, please share your concerns with the designated church official for resolution.

Christ Church seeks to nurture a family environment, thus we begin our day with a morning prayer. We want to do more than work together...we also want to pray together.

YOU ARE A VALUED MEMBER OF THIS STAFF...MAY THE GRACE AND PEACE OF OUR LORD ABIDE IN YOU.

MISSION STATEMENT

"Your Mission Statement Here"

VISION STATEMENT

"Your Vision Statement Here"

CHURCH HISTORY

Christ Church

"A brief summary of your church's history here"

Church Covenant

"Your Church Covenant Here"

EMPLOYEE OBLIGATIONS

Each employee is required to:

- Know the policies and procedures and application in their case
- Seek information from their supervisor in case of doubt or misunderstanding on the application of the policies and procedures
- Adhere to the policies and procedures
- Be aware of the consequences of violation of the laws, rules, and regulations regarding policies of Christ Church

EMPLOYEE EXPECTATIONS

Members of Christ Church staff are expected to:

- Know and support the Mission and Vision of Christ Church
- Plan and organize work assignments to facilitate productivity
- Provide courteous service that represents the spirit of Christ Church
- Maintain constructive and loving relationships with the staff, members of Christ Church, and the community
- Consistently meet deadlines
- Motivate their best efforts through self-set goals
- Contribute to accomplishments/success of team/church-wide assignments/activities
- Keep supervisor (pastor as necessary) informed concerning work in progress and any challenges encountered. Avoid surprises
- Demonstrate professionalism by maintaining an attitude of wanting to do a first class job in a first class (quality) way

All Rise: Church Staffing
Building an Effective Ministry Staff

STAFF STRUCTURE/EMPLOYMENT

Ministerial Staff

Ministers who have been officially appointed by the Senior Pastor and who have been formally ordained, licensed, or commissioned to preach or minister.

Administrative / Managerial Staff

These staff members are non-minister employees who serve in a key administrative or managerial position.

Support Staff

These staff positions consist of the support functions, which service the numerous ministries of the church.

Employment Classifications

ALL NEW HIRES WILL SERVE A PROBATIONARY PERIOD OF 180 DAYS (6 MONTHS)

- Exempt – Salaried employees
- Non-exempt-Hourly employees
- Regular Full-time – 32-40 hours per week
- Regular Part-time – 20 hours per week or less
- Internship Program – employees serving under the pastor's supervision
- Temporary Full-time –employees who work a minimum of 32 hours per week for a specific period
- Temporary Part – time –part time employees who work 20 hours per week or less for a period not to exceed 12 months
- Contract/temporary on – call employees who work as needed

Compensation

- Pay period – Bi-weekly pay period (26 pay periods annually)
- Timesheets/time cards – all non-exempt hourly employees are required to use time cards
- All overtime and compensatory time requires prior approval
- Overtime applies only to non-exempt employees
- Time and a half pay is granted to employees whose work exceeds 40 hours per week
- Overtime is intended to be a vehicle to resolve emergencies or abnormal work schedules
- Compensatory time may be used to adjust employee work schedule

WORKPLACE GUIDELINES

Personal Appearance and Dress Code

Employees are expected to groom themselves in a manner appropriate to the occasion and their duties.

Open Door Policy

One of the foremost goals of Christ Church is to ensure that each employee has a way to express problems, opinions or suggestions. For all administrative matters, the employee should talk with the immediate supervisor first. If the supervisor cannot resolve an issue, the supervisor should refer the employee to the next highest supervisor level for resolution.

Tardiness and Absence

The offices of the church are open Monday through Friday from 9:00 a.m. to 5:00 p.m.). If an employee is unable to report to work for any reason, he/she must call the church office no later than 9:00 a.m. Employee should talk directly to his/here supervisor. Leaving a message is not acceptable. If the supervisor is not in the office at the time of the call, the Church Administrator should be contacted. If neither is available, employee may then leave a message requesting a return call.

An employee who is tardy or absent excessively or shows a consistent pattern of absence, whether excused or unexcused, will be subject to disciplinary action, which may include termination.

Break and Lunch Periods

Non-exempt employees are provided one (1) fifteen (15) minute break period for each four hours of work. Break periods should be taken near the middle of the four (4) hour work period. A thirty (30) minute unpaid lunch period is provided for non-exempt employees who work more than five (5) hours in a workday. However, employees who do not work more than six (6) hours in a workday may choose to waive their right to a lunch period.

All break times will be established by supervisors. Break periods may not be accumulated to reduce working hours or to provide time off for personal business. No work should be performed during the break and lunch periods.

Grievances and Complaints

Employees who have grievances or complaints regarding church policies, procedures or organizational structure should discuss them with their immediate supervisor. Discussions should be made within two (2) consecutive workdays. If the employee feels a grievance or complaint is unresolved by the supervisor, the employee should submit the concern in writing to the Church Administrator. A review will be conducted and appropriate actions taken within five (5) working days. If the employee is still not satisfied, he/she may place the concern in writing to the Personnel Committee. The Committee will review the matter with the Senior Pastor and provide a response. The final decision is made by the Senior Pastor.

Employee Family Members

We thank God for the spouses and children of our staff and we always desire that they place their family first before the ministry. Staff must remain sensitive to Christ Church position of responsibility with children. Children are not allowed on church property without proper supervision. The church will not assume responsibility for a child left unattended. Employees should not get in the habit of allowing extended visits from children, spouses, or other family members during work hours.

Personal Mail

Due to the large amounts of mail the church receives, it is important that mail of a personal nature be delivered to the employee's home address.

Counseling Sessions

Christ Church is committed to protecting the integrity of our staff and the reputation of our church. Scripture stipulates that church leaders are to be "above reproach", and that even the "appearance" of wrongdoing should be avoided. Therefore, the following counseling guidelines have been established for all staff members to follow:

- Never visit the opposite sex in a home environment
- Never counsel the opposite sex alone in a church office or room
- Never counsel the opposite sex more than once without the counselee's mate present. Refer them to the Marriage Counseling Ministry
- Never go to breakfast, lunch or dinner alone with the opposite sex
- Never kiss any church member or church guest of the opposite sex
- Never discuss detailed sexual problems with the opposite sex. Refer them to a same sex ministry (i.e. Women's Ministry, Men's Ministry, etc.)

- Never discuss personal marriage problems with any church member or church guest of the opposite sex
- Never drive alone in a car of the opposite sex
- Use church Secretaries and open/glass viewing rooms as protective measures

Access To and Removal of Church Property

It is critical that Christ Church has access at all times to church property. As a result, the church reserves the right to access employee offices, work stations, filing cabinets, desk, credenzas, and any other church property at its discretion, with or without advance notice or consent. Such access would also include records, documents, files, schedules, ledgers, etc.

No property is to be loaned or removed from the church grounds without the approval through the Church Administrator's office.

Issuance of Church Property and Equipment

The Church Administrator will issue keys to exterior doors and/or offices of the church to appropriate employees. Church issued keys should not be used by anyone except the employee to whom they are issued. An employee should never duplicate church keys.

Use of Church Telephone

Church leadership realizes that it may be necessary for employees to occasionally make and receive personal calls on church telephones. However, such calls should be held to a minimum. Such personal calls should be made, whenever possible, during scheduled break and lunch periods. The employee is expected to inform each of their family members of these guidelines. Unavoidable lengthy personal calls should be cleared through their supervisor and time appropriately adjusted on their time sheet.

Use of church telephones to make personal long-distance calls is not allowed unless prior approval is received from the Church Administrator's office.

Use of Church Computers (including email usage)

The purpose of these guidelines is to maintain the integrity of Christ Church's computer network. Understanding of, and abiding by these guidelines, is essential to ensure that the system can be used without impeaching its integrity.

Church computers are only to be used for church business. Personal use and maintenance of personal data on church computers are not allowed.

The use of personal software will not be allowed. Loading personal software is the number one means of introducing viruses into a computer network.

Computer software purchased by Christ Church is owned by the church and should not be copied or installed on employee home computers.

All computers owned by Christ Church will be subject to periodic inspections for compliance with these guidelines.

Failure to comply with these guidelines could result in immediate termination.

Vacation

Employees who have worked a total of the following hours will be entitled to vacation as follows:

- 6 months or less   0 weeks
- 7-12 month   1 week
- 1-4 years   2 weeks
- 5-14 years   3 weeks
- 15-24 years   4 weeks
- 25 years   5 weeks

Holidays

Ten (10) holidays are observed

- New Year's Day
- Martin Luther King, Jr. (MLK) Birthday
- Easter (Monday Following Easter Sunday)
- Memorial Day
- Independence Day
- Labor Day
- Thanksgiving Day
- Friday after Thanksgiving
- Christmas Eve
- Christmas Day

Leave of Absence

Personal leave (without pay up to 30 days)

Family care and medical leave (up to 6 weeks without pay)

Bereavement leave for immediate family (3 workdays or 5 if out of state)

Spouse	Children
Parent	Brother
Sister	Grandparents

Or relative that resides with employee

Jury Duty

A leave of absence will be granted for employees to serve on jury duty. Full-time employees who are called to serve on jury duty will be paid their regular wages during the time they are called to serve.

Military Leave

Employees who are required, as members of the National Guard or a reserve unit, to attend a training period not exceeding two weeks will be granted the necessary time off and will be paid the difference in the amount they receive from the government for this training (less travel allowance) and their regular wages for that period. These employees must present a statement from the commanding officer as to the length of training and the amount of compensation (less travel allowance) received for the period of training.

Workers' Compensation Leave

A leave of absence will be granted whenever there is a work-related illness or injury.

Sick Leave

Employees who have completed at least 90 days of continuous service will be eligible to participate in the church's sick leave program. This plan provides for both job continuance and pay in the event of an employee absence for certain periods of time for reasons of illness, injury, or disability which were not work related.

Employees accrue one (1/2) day per month sick leave.

Cafeteria Plan (Insurance)

All full-time employees qualify to participate in this plan. The plan becomes effective after 30 days of employment. Through the Cafeteria Plan, each employee may receive a monthly allowance to use to pay for any of the following benefits:

- Health insurance
- Eye examination
- Life insurance

Each employee is free to choose the insurance coverage his/her family may need. Insurance premiums are deducted from the employee's monthly allowance.

Detailed descriptions for each of the above benefits and information pamphlets regarding each of the insurance options can be obtained in the Church Administrator's Office.

Anniversary Recognition

Anniversary Recognition (All Full-Time Staff)

At quarterly staff meetings, all anniversaries for the current quarter will be acknowledged. Those with five, ten, etc. year anniversaries will be given service awards.

The Church Administrator is responsible for notifying the church Media about anniversary recognition. An Employee News Memorandum (Form No. 9-09) will be used to initiate the publishing of such recognitions.

Retirement (Annuity) Participation

From the employee's date of hire, beginning the first day of the following month, the church will contribute 3% of the employee's annualized base salary to the church's 403(b) tax sheltered annuity. The employee also has the option to complete a Salary Reduction Agreement (Form No. 7-11) and have an additional amount withheld from their pay. Limits do apply.

Employees will be required to complete needed forms to establish this annuity arrangement. Information will also be provided to the employee from the Church Administrator's office, regarding the tax-sheltered annuity.

Social Security

The employer's portion of Social Security and Medicare taxes (FICA) will be provided for all non-minister employees.

Workers' Compensation Insurance

Every employees of Christ Church is automatically covered by Workers' Compensation Insurance at the time of employment. The church pays the entire premium for this coverage.

As required in the church's Workplace Safety and Security Policy, all employees are required to report any type of work-related injury or illness to their supervisor, as soon as it occurs, regardless of how minor the injury or sickness may be. The Church Administrator should be notified immediately when any work-related or illness occurs.

PERFORMANCE STANDARDS

"On the contrary we worked night and day, laboring and toiling so that we would not be a burden to any of you. We did this, not because we do not have the right to such help, but in order to make ourselves a model for you to follow."   2 Thessalonians 3:8, 9

His master replied, "Well done, good and faithful servant! You have been faithful with few things: I will put you in charge of many things."   Matthew 25:21

"So he called him in and asked him, "What is this I hear about you? Give an account of your management, because you cannot be manager any longer." Luke 16:2

Statement of Policies and Procedures

It is the church's policy to conduct performance reviews with employees on a regular scheduled basis as a means of fostering employees' development and motivating employees to reach their full potential.

Work Performance

Employees may be disciplined, up to and including termination, for poor work performance as determined by their supervisors, Church Administrator and/or the Senior Pastor.

Examples of Poor Work Performance are as follows, but not limited to:

Below average work in quality or quantity

Poor attitude, including rudeness, lack of cooperation, acts of dissention within

Excessive absenteeism, tardiness, or abuse of break and lunch privileges

Failure to follow supervisory instructions or abide by church policies and procedures

Misconduct and/or Behavior

Employees may also be disciplined, up to and including termination, for misconduct and/or unacceptable behavior. Examples of misconduct are as follows, but are not limited to:

- Acts of insubordination
- Abuse, misuse, theft, or the unauthorized possession or removal of church property or the personal property of others
- Falsifying or making a material omission on church records, reports, or other documents, including payroll, personnel, and employment records
- Divulging confidential church information to unauthorized persons

- Disorderly conduct on church property, including fighting or attempted bodily injury, the use of profane, abusive, or threatening language toward others, or possession of a weapon
- Violation of any law adversely affecting the church, or conviction in court of any crime that may cause the employee to be regarded as unsuitable for continued employment
- Violation of the church's alcohol, drugs and controlled substance policy
- Marking or signing the time records of another employee or knowingly allowing another employee to mark or sign their time record
- Any immoral conduct which bring reproach upon the name of the Lord Jesus Christ and our church

Disciplinary Action

Whenever disciplinary action is needed, it will always be done in a spirit of restoration. When an employee has been counseled without results, the following progressive actions may be performed. However, certain cases may warrant only one or two of the following steps, while others might require all three steps to be followed, they are:

- Informal Oral reminder
- Formal Oral Reprimand Notice
- Final Warning Notice
- Supervisor, Senior Pastor and Personnel Committee will review dismissal notice

Position Description

All approved personnel positions (full-time or part-time) must have a current Position Description on file with the Personnel Committee prior to hiring an applicant. The position description serves as an organizational and ministerial aid for identifying and delegating responsibilities.

Performance Evaluations

Employees are expected to conscientiously perform their duties of Church Church and the public, respond readily to the direction of their supervisors, and conduct their relations with fellow employees in a manner, which does not cause dissension or discord.

Employees will receive their first written performance evaluation after approximately 6 months from the end of the probationary period and approximately every year thereafter. The employee's immediate supervisor will prepare the evaluations. If an employee reports to more than one supervisor, both supervisors should be involved in the review process.

The purpose of the performance evaluation is to inform the employee how well they are doing, while considering their length of time in the position in relation to the performance requirements for the position.

TERMINATIONS

Voluntary Termination

A voluntary termination is a termination that is initiated by the employee.

Involuntary Termination

An involuntary termination is a termination that is initiated by church management for reason other than changing ministry conditions.

The church may compensate dismissed employees with a salary equivalent equaling two weeks of the employee's annual base salary.

SALARY AND WAGE ADMINISTRATION

Christ Church will provide a fair, consistent and equitable method of determining rates of pay for its salary and hourly employees based upon the responsibilities, skills and qualifications required for each position. This method will also utilize objective criteria for the proper placement of each employee within employment classifications and applicable pay scales, and allow for the establishment of salary and hourly increases based upon the results of each employee's performance evaluation.

Cost Of Living (COL) as recommended by the budget committee

*"For the scripture says "do not muzzle the ox while it is treading out the grain",
and "the worker deserves his wages."*   I Timothy 5:18

*"So I will come near to you for judgment, I will be quick to testify...against those
who defraud laborers of their wages..."*   Malachi 3:5

Internet Resources:

Corporate forms and resolutions: http://www.amazon.com/Corporate-Forms-Kit-Rev-disk/dp/1574100572#reader_1574100572

Church Tax Laws: www.churchlawandtax.com/aboutus.php

Church Accounting and Taxes: www.chitwoods.com

Church Business Administration, Salary, Survey Etc.: www.nacba.net/Pages/Home.aspx

Church Staffing Resource and Job Descriptions: www.ChurchStaffing.com

IRS Forms: www.irs.gov/formspubs/ Church Forms: www.friezconsulting.com/index.php?option=com_content&task=view&i

Building an Effective Ministry Staff

Sample Dance Ministry Request Form

Ministry Name _____

Contact Person _____

Telephone _____ Email _____

Event _____ Date _____

Time _____ Location _____

Place a check next to the group requested to dance in ministry:

Children Ages 5-7 _____

Youth Ages 12-17 _____

Adults 18 - Over _____

Soloist _____ Praise Dance _____

Event Colors _____

Stage: Yes _____ No _____

Practice site available: Yes _____ No _____

Rehearsal Date _____

Additional Information: _____
_____
_____
_____
_____

Building an Effective Ministry Staff

Sample Prayer Request Form

PRAYER REQUEST / PRAISE REPORT

"Be anxious for nothing, but in everything by prayer and supplication, with thanksgiving, let your requests be made known to God; and the peace of God, which surpasses all understanding, will guard your hearts and minds through Christ Jesus." (Philippians 4: 6-7)

Please check one:

☐ *Please pray for*   ☐ *Praise Report for*

Name: _____   Date: _____

Address: _____

City / State / Zip _____

Check one:

☐ New prayer request

☐ Update to previous prayer request

Is this person a member of The GPGBC? ☐*Yes* ☐*No* ☐*Not sure*   ☐ Praise report of previous request

Is this person a Christian? ☐*Yes* ☐*No* ☐*Not sure*

Can praise report be share to exhort the church body? ☐*Yes* ☐*No*

_____

_____

_____

Person making request: Is this person making the request a member of The GPGBC? ☐*Yes* ☐*No*

Name: _____

Address: _____

City: _____ State: _____ Zip: _____

Phone: (h) _____ (w) _____

Relationship to person prayed for:

☐ *Self*   ☐ *Family Member*   ☐ *Friend*   ☐ *Other*

This form has been distributed to:

_____   _____

_____   _____

Sample Death and

Bereavement Form

Death - Bereavement Form

Date _____ Time (:) Called received by: _____

Caller Name _____ | Relation to Deceased _____ | Telephone No. _____

Card(s) Sent ☐ | Flowers Orders ☐   Date Ordered: _____

Contact Telephone Numbers

Contact Name: _____

Deceased Information ☐ Member   ☐ Non-Member

Home No. _____

Work No. _____

Name _____

Other Contact No. _____

Home Address _____

Mortuary Information

Name _____   Telephone No. _____

Mortuary Address _____

Funeral Services Information (i.e., Church)

Name of Facility _____

Facility Address _____

Wake: Yes ☐ No ☐   Wake Location: _____

Building an Effective Ministry Staff

Sample Cash Collection Form

CASH COLLECTION FORM

Please do not hold cash or checks. All cash should be turned in weekly by each Sunday.

Date: _____   Activity: _____

Ministry/Dept: _____   Signature: _____

Completed by: _____   Signature: _____
(Print Name)

CASH	Quantity	$ Amount	CHECKS Name	$	Check #
100's				$	
50's				$	
20's				$	
10's				$	
5's				$	
1's				$	
Quarters				$	
Dimes				$	
Nickels				$	
Pennies				$	
TOTAL CASH			TOTAL CHECKS	$	
				$	

List of Individuals with Cash Donations	Amount
	$
	$
	$
	$
	$
	$
	$
	$
Amount from attached list (if applicable)	$
Total Cash from Individuals	$

TOTAL CASH $ _____

TOTAL CHECKS $ _____

Less: Start up Cash Change $ _____

GROSS DEPOSIT $ _____

Submitted by: _____
Print Name: _____

Funds Received by: _____
Church Administrator's Office

Funds Verified by: _____
Finance Room/Print Name: _____
Date: _____

Sample Copy Request Form

COPY REQUEST FORM

Today's Date : _____

Ministry _____

Account # _____

Submitted By _____

Phone No. _____

Date and Time Needed _____

Number of Originals _____

Number of Copies _____

One-sided ____
Two-sided ____

Collated ____
Grouped ____
Stapled ____
Book Style ____

Color Copies ____
Color Paper ____
3 Holed Punch ____
Comb Bound ____

SPECIAL INSTRUCTIONS
_____
_____
_____
_____
_____
_____
_____

Return to _____ Phone No. _____

Office Hours 9:00am to 4:00pm Monday thru Friday

Thank you for your cooperation.
The Church Staff Completed_____

PLEASE COMPLETE THIS FORM AND RETURN TO CHURCH ADMINISTRATOR 7 DAYS IN ADVANCE OF DATE NEEDED. THIS WILL PROVIDE SUFFICIENT TIME TO COORDINATE AND COMPLETE YOUR REQUEST. BE MINDFUL THAT IF THIS FORM IS NOT RETURNED IN A TIMELY MANNER THAT THERE IS NO GUARANTEE THAT YOU WILL HAVE THE COPIES YOU NEED.

Building an Effective Ministry Staff

Sample Van Request Form

VAN REQUEST FORM

Ministry/Auxiliary _____

Date of road trip _____

Destination of road trip _____

Contact Person _____
(Secretary of Auxiliary or designated driver)

Number of passengers _____   Time of departure _____

Report time _____   Number of days _____

Purpose of trip _____
_____

Special Instructions:
_____
_____
_____

President of Ministry/Auxiliary _____

Request Forms should be submitted to the Special Projects Coordinator a minimum of four-
teen (14) business days prior to date van is needed.

Building an Effective Ministry Staff

Sample Room Reservation Request Form

Room Reservation Request Form

Today's Date _____

Ministry/Auxiliary _____

Date of request _____ Time _____

Contact Person(s) _____

Phone _____

Description of event _____

_____

Room arrangement request _____

_____

_____

_____

Location desired _____

Number of attendees _____

Signature _____

****

Room assigned _____

Program Office _____

Building an Effective Ministry Staff

Sample Photography and
Video Request Form

PHOTOGRAPHY / VIDEO MINISTRY
REQUEST FORM

Date Received: _____

Ministry / Auxiliary Name: _____

Contact Name: _____   Phone: _____

                                        Work: _____

Alternate Contact: _____   Phone: _____

Services Needed: _____ Photos

_____ Portraits

_____ Video

Date Services needed: _____

Times services needed: _____

Location required for services _____

Occasion: _____

(Example:Retreat, Banquets, Breakfast, Forum, Weddings, Funerals, Lock-ins, Get-Away, Baby Dedications, Anniversaries, Special Events, and Receptions, etc.)

Type of film: _____ Color

(Takes one (1) week to develop.)

                      _____ Black & White

LOCATION ASSIGNED FOR PROJECT: _____

ALL REQUEST MUST BE SUBMITTED ONE (1) MONTH IN ADVANCE TO THE PROGRAM AND FACILITY COODINATOR.

Date Assigned _____

Building an Effective Ministry Staff

{CHURCH NAME}
FINANCE OFFICE - SAMPLE COUNT SHEET

SPEAKER: _____

SERVICE: ☐ A.M.   ☐ REVIVAL   DAY: _____

            ☐ P.M.   ☐ MUSICAL   DATE: _____

            ☐ MID-WEEK   ☐ OTHER: _____

☐ TITHES   ☐ OFFERINGS   ☐ BUILDING FUND   ☐ MISSIONS   ☐ BENEVOLENCE   ☐ OTHER: _____

A)	CASH	AMT.		B)	STRAPS	NO.	AMT.
	100's	$_____			$2000 x ____ =		$_____
	50's	_____			1000 x ____ =		_____
	20's	_____			500 x ____ =		_____
	10's	_____			250 x ____ =		_____
	5's	_____			200 x ____ =		_____
	2's	_____			100 x ____ =		_____
	1's	_____			50 x ____ =		_____
					Loose Cash =		_____
(1)	SUB-TOTAL	$_____		(1)	SUB-TOTAL		$_____

	COINS	AMT.			ROLLED COINS	NO.	AMT.
	Dollars	$_____			$10.00 x ____ =		$_____
	Half-Dollars	_____			5.00 x ____ =		_____
	Quarters	_____			2.50 x ____ =		_____
	Dimes	_____			.50 x ____ =		_____
	Nickels	_____			____ x ____ =		_____
	Pennies	_____			Loose Coins =		_____
(2)	SUB-TOTAL	$_____		(2)	SUB-TOTAL		$_____
(3)	CHECKS	$_____		(3)	CHECKS		$_____
	TOTALS A (1+2+3)	$_____			TOTALS B (1+2+3)		$_____

TOTAL TO BE DEPOSITED IN BANK AND VERIFIED BY BANK DEPOSIT SLIP

COUNTERS SIGNATURE(S): _____

_____

_____

SAMPLE LETTER

**"Notification to Minister of
Housing Allowance by the Church"**

DATE

Reverend John Doe, Pastor
Heavenly Host Church
333 Beinformed Way
Anywhere, GA 38333

RE: Notification by Employer

Dear

This is to advise you that the meeting of the Board of Trustees of _____
_____ was held on _____ in
reference to your parsonage allowance for the year _____. **The board officials
designated and fixed the amount of $_____ as your salary.**

Accordingly, $_____ of the total payment to you during the _____year will
constitute parsonage allowance and the balance will constitute compensation under **Section
107 of the Internal Revenue Code which states that a minister is allowed to exclude
from gross income the rental allowance paid as part of rental compensation to rent or
provide a home.**

You should keep an accurate record of your expenditures to rent or provide a home in order
to be able to substantiate any amount excluded from gross income in filing your Federal
Income Tax Return.

Sincerely,

Building an Effective Ministry Staff

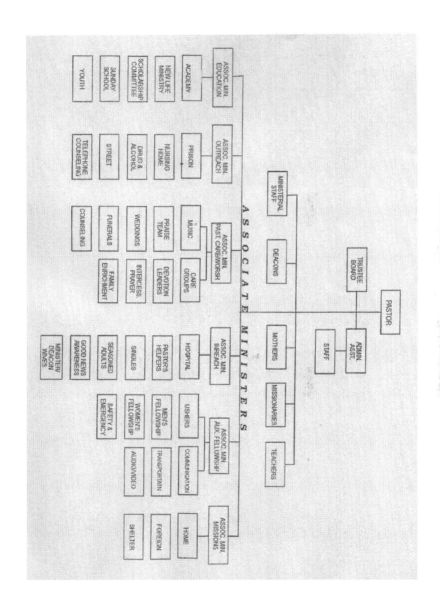

Building an Effective Ministry Staff

Sample Floral Request Form

Receiver: _____

Deliver to:

Hospital : _____
_____
_____

Funeral : _____
Home   _____
_____

Home :   _____
_____
_____

Sample Benevolent Assistance Form

Social Security No.: _____   Spouse's Social Security No.: _____

Date: _____   ☐ Own   ☐ Rent   ☐ Other _____

Name: _____   Phone ( ) _____

Address: _____

City: _____   State: _____   Zipcode: _____

Age: _____   ☐ Single   ☐ Married   ☐ Divorced   ☐ Separated   ☐ Widow

Spouse's Name: _____   Spouse's Employment: _____

Children's Ages: _____

Needs: ☐ Food   ☐ Clothing   ☐ Shelter   ☐ Rent / Mortgage   ☐ Utilities _____

☐ Transient   ☐ Other (Explain) _____

Deadline: _____   Amount Needed: $ _____

Have you been helped previously by this Church?   ☐ Yes   ☐ No

What did you receive? _____   When? _____

Other organizations you have applied to for this need? _____

Please explain the circumstances which brought about this need. _____

_____

_____

Home Church: _____   Phone ( ) _____

Church Address: _____

Pastor's Name: _____   Phone ( ) _____

Doctor's Name: _____   Phone ( ) _____

Landlord's Name: _____   Phone ( ) _____

Landlord's Address: _____

Monthly Average Cost: Mortgage/Rent $ _____   Auto $ _____   Electric $ _____

Water $ _____   Phone $ _____   Medical $ _____   Gas $ _____

Building an Effective Ministry Staff

Other (Explain) _____

If you are requesting a bill payment, please supply the following information. (For more than one bill, please attach the additional information):

Company Name: _____

Phone ( ) _____ Contact Person: _____

Address: _____

City: _____ State: _____ Zip Code: _____

Account Number: _____ Total Amount Due $ _____

Amount Required $ _____

List Two Personal References:

Name: _____ Phone ( ) _____

Address: _____

City: _____ State: _____ Zip Code: _____

Name: _____ Phone ( ) _____

Address: _____

City: _____ State: _____ Zip Code: _____

Other Sources Willing to Assist with this Need:

Name: _____ Phone ( ) _____ Amount $ _____

Name: _____ Phone ( ) _____ Amount $ _____

Name: _____ Phone ( ) _____ Amount $ _____

Do Not Write Below This Line – For Church Use Only

Date Application Received in this Office: _____

Information from Community Help Line (Contact Name) _____

Disapproved _____ Reason: _____

Approved _____ Approved by: _____

Date Paid: _____ Amount $ _____ Check No. _____

Written by: _____ Payable to: _____

Send to: _____

Address: _____

City: _____ State: _____ Zip Code: _____

Comments: _____

Signatures: (At Least Two Committee Members or One Member and Pastor)

_____

Building an Effective Ministry Staff

Sample Church Property Loan Form

Furniture/Equipment Loan Authorization

Permission is hereby granted to (name) _____

to borrow (list item(s)) _____

_____

_____

Model No. (if applicable): _____

_____

_____

Serial No. (if applicable): _____

_____

_____

The above items to be returned and checked in on (date) _____

_____   _____

James D. McWhorter, Church Administrator   Signature of Borrower

_____   _____

Maintenance Personnel (Checked Out)   Name of Borrower (Please Print)

_____   _____

Date   Borrower's Phone Number or Cell Phone Number

_____   _____

Maintenance Personnel (Checked In)   Date

_____

Date

Building an Effective Ministry Staff

Sample Special Supplies Order Form

Date of Request _____

Ministry _____

Ordered By _____

Vendor _____ Budget Line No. _____

Qty.	Catalog Page No.	Item No.	Description	Unit Price	Total Price

TOTAL (This page.) $_____

Approved By _____ Date _____

Sample Vehicle Checklist Form

river's Last Name _____ Driver's First Name _____
lease PRINT
ate: _____ Time in _____ (AM/PM) Time out _____ (AM\PM)

estination _____

ehicle Used   Milege Out   Milege In
- Van
- 15 Passenger
- 25 Passenger

proximately Gas Reading
as Out   Full   3/4   1/2   1/4   E   Gas In   Full   3/4   1/2   1/4   E

EXTERIOR INSPECTION
Place an (✓) mark in each box to indicate inspection is complete.
Place an (x) mark to indicate a problem with vehicle.

OUT	IN	ITEM	OUT	IN	ITEM
		Front Left Tire/ Hubcap/Lugs			Right Rear Tire/Hubcap/Lugs
		Door			Doors/Body
		Mirror			Mirror
		Rear Left Tire			Front Right Tire/Hubcap/Lug
		Rear Bumper			Front Bumper
		Tail Lights			Head Lights
		Tag			Fluid Leaks
		Doors			Wiper Blades
		Other			Other

Give Brief Damage Description _____

OUT	IN	INTERIOR	OUT	IN	INTERIOR
		Dash Fluid Gauges			Seat belts
		Head Lighting			Paper/Debris
		Floor			Spills/Odor
		Give Brief Description (other)			

Building an Effective Ministry Staff

About the Authors

Dr. William E. Flippin, Sr. is a native of Nashville, Tennessee. Dr. Flippin has earned a Bachelor of Arts degree in Mathematics and Business Administration from Fisk University in Nashville, Tennessee. In addition, Dr. Flippin holds a Master of Divinity (Cum Laude) from Candler School of Theology at Emory University in Atlanta, Georgia. Dr. Flippin earned a Doctorate of Ministry from McCormick Theological Seminary in Chicago, Illinois. Dr. Flippin is currently a Certified Life Transformational Coach and also a Certified Leadership Coach Trainer where his main objective is to *raise leaders*. Currently, he faithfully serves as Senior Pastor of The Greater Piney Grove Baptist Church ("The Grove") in Atlanta, Georgia. Since 1990, Pastor Flippin has led The Greater Piney Grove to a unique sense of mission and outreach. Recently, "The Grove" purchased 22-additional acres on their church property to secure a total of 50 acres which is named The Promise Land at Eastlake.

He also serves as the Founder and CEO of The Flippin Legacy Ministries, Inc, The Pearl Initiative, Inc. (Non-Profit); and Pearls of Great Price Ministries, Inc (For-Profit). He is the author of five books: In My Father's House, Order in the Church, Order in the Pulpit, God's Order, Vision 20/20. Dr. Flippin has been married for over thirty-seven years to Sylvia Taylor Flippin, who is an instructional coach for the DeKalb County Board of Education. Dr. and Mrs. Flippin are the proud parents of one daughter, Miss Sylvia Joi, and three sons who continue the family legacy of preaching: William E. Flippin, Jr. (Kedra S.), Richard C. Flippin, Joseph C. T. Flippin (Kendall D.) Flippin

James D. McWhorter serves as the current church administrator of The Greater Piney Grove Baptist Church and has served formerly at Cathedral of Faith Church of God in Christ, both in Atlanta, GA, serving in this capacity for over 32 years. He has conducted numerous seminars and workshops to train and equip church leaders and laity in various aspects of church administration, staffing, stewardship, and financial integrity. He has also been privileged to minister and train pastors and church leaders in Kenya, East Africa and Ghana and Nigeria, West Africa.

He and his wife of 41 years are the proud parents of three children, James III, Eric and Camille and five grandchildren.

Other Reading Material God's

Order: Order in the Church God's

Order: Order in the Pulpit

20/20 Vision for the Victor

All can be purchased at Amazon.com

36150574R00089

Made in the USA
Charleston, SC
26 November 2014